MATH SUPERSTARS™

CRITTER ADDITION
LEVEL 3

ESSENTIALS

By Robert Stanek
BESTSELLING AUTHOR

LISTEN TO THE BUGVILLE CRITTERS AT BEDTIME... AUDIO BOOKS AVAILABLE AT WWW.AUDIBLE.COM

5th Edition, Copyright © 2020 Robert Stanek. BUGVILLE CRITTERS, MATH SUPERSTARS, CRITTER ESSENTIALS and all associated logos and designs are trademarks and/or registered trademarks of Robert Stanek.

Published by Bugville Learning and Big Blue Sky Press.

Bugville Learning

Bugville Learning is a creation of Robert Stanek, who also writes as William Stanek. Mr. Stanek wrote professionally for over 30 years. In 2020, he celebrated the publication of his 250th book and 20 millionth reader. That's a lot of books, a lot of years of writing, and a lot of readers, making him one of the most prolific and popular writers of all time. His books have been published and/or distributed by every major US publisher, and over 100 other publishers globally.

Writing as Robert Stanek, he was the first breakout author of the digital publishing revolution. Writing as William Stanek, he is credited with transforming the computer writing industry with his plain language style. A style that Microsoft eventually adopted for its own. Millions of training courses taught by Microsoft and others used his words as their foundations.

Learn more about the author at www.williamrstanek.com.

BUGVILLE CRITTERS

Over100
Bugville Books

ROBERT STANEK

15 Years
3 million readers

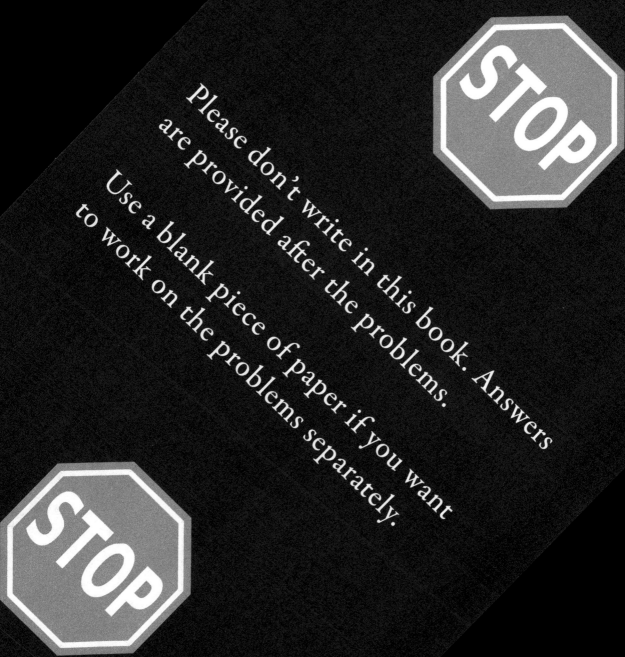

Please don't write in this book. Answers are provided after the problems.

Use a blank piece of paper if you want to work on the problems separately.

Please don't write in this book. Answers are provided after the problems.

Use a blank piece of paper if you want to work on the problems separately.

Welcome to Math Superstars!

Our selection of activities and problems provides a fun and easy approach to building math skills. This book contains math problems presented as with pictures and words. Questions and answers are provided on separate pages.

Each question page presents a math problem using three different approaches:

1) **As a math equation.** Math equations are presented as they'd be written to solve a problem. For rapid review, you can use the math equations like you would use flash cards.

2) **As a word problem.** Word problems are presented using verbal cues to help arrive at the answer. Solving word problems requires critical thinking that can help to build more advanced math skills.

3) **As a visual problem.** Visual problems use objects as counters to help demonstrate how to arrive at the answer. This approach is best for beginners and any child having difficulty with a particular problem.

Includes trivia and review pages to help develop related skills. Reinforces learned skills with repetition.

Notes for Parents & Educators

Each answer page provides the answer for each of the ways the problem is presented. (Look for the spelled-out form of the number in the answer to the word problem. As your child's skills improve, have your child point out the number and its spelled-out counterpart.)

To make learning easier, this book is divided into sections. Each section contains several math problems and their answers. Use break pages to help track when it's time to stop for a while or the day.

To begin using this book, turn the page and follow along. When you come to a question page, turn your book so that your child can read the math equation. Point to the math equation. Ask your child to tell you the correct answer and then turn the page to show the answer. Children can also work independently.

Tips for Absolute Beginners

For absolute beginners, point to the math equation and then to the visual problem. Have your child count the objects. Reinforce the count of each object grouping by repeating the group count when your child says it. For example, with $5+3$, say, "Yes, five!" after your child counts from one to five, and then "Hurray, eight!" when your child finishes the count.

As your child's skills improve, reinforce the connection to the math equation by referring to the group count rather than the object count. For example, with $5+3$, say, "Yes, five!" after your child counts from one to five, and then "Yes, three more is eight!" when your child finishes the count. Afterward, point to the equation.

Note that objects are grouped for easier counting in multiples. As your child's skills improve, you may want to occasionally work on counting in multiples, such as by threes or fours, rather than by ones, and then adding to this count as necessary to reach the answer. This approach helps build essential connective skills. For example, with $10+3$, encourage counting by threes and then adding one to this count.

Tips for Advancing Superstars

For advancing superstars, focus on the word problem and the math equation. Read the word problem aloud, or have your child read the word problem. Use the math equation as necessary to help give the word problem context. As your child advances, focus increasingly on the word problem.

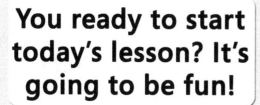
You ready to start today's lesson? It's going to be fun!

Sure thing, after we finish riding our bikes.

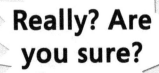

MATH SUPER STARS

You **add** to find out how many things there are in all. Example: 12 + 5 = 17.

Here we are adding the numbers 12 and 5. We use a + sign to show this.

17 is how many we have in all. This is called the **sum**. We use an = sign to show the sum.

Math sentences are called equations. Equations can be written two ways:

$$12 + 9 = 21$$

$$\begin{array}{r} 12 \\ +9 \\ \hline 21 \end{array}$$

MATH SUPER STARS

When you have groups of things, you can count them to determine the sum. Count the skateboards to determine how many there are:

+ =

The answer is:

1 4 7 10
2 5 + 8 11 = 12
3 6 9 12

But also think about how many things are in each group:

6 boards + 6 boards = 12 boards

$$\begin{array}{r} 10 \\ +9 \\ \hline 19 \end{array}$$

There are 19 skaters at the party. Cool, nineteen.

 $= \underline{19}$

$$11 + 7$$

BREAK

BREAK TEASERS

Would you add or subtract the numbers 7 and 2 to get 9?

Add 3 to 27. What do you get?

BREAK

ANSWERS

Would you add or subtract the numbers 7 and 2 to get 9?	**Add (7 + 2 = 9)**
Add 3 to 27. What do you get?	**30 (27 + 3 = 30)**

MATH SUPER STARS

Count the number of boats in each group.

MATH SUPER STARS

Say the answers out loud.

2

4

6

8

10

You are counting by 2s!

BREAK

BREAK TEASERS

Lass collected 10 colorful leaves for the Fall Leaf wall. Buster collected 7 leaves. How many leaves in all?

Start with 12 and count ahead 3. What number did you get?

BREAK

ANSWERS

Lass collected 10 colorful leaves for the Fall Leaf wall. Buster collected 7 leaves. How many leaves in all?	17 (10 + 7 = 17)
Start with 12 and count ahead 3. What number did you get?	14 (12, 13, 14)

MATH SUPER STARS

Count the number of bikes in each group.

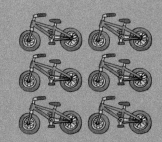

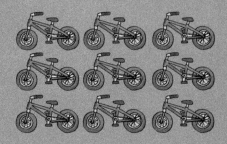

MATH SUPER STARS

Say the answers out loud.

3

6

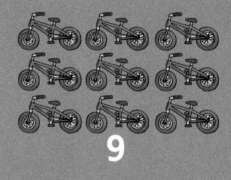

9

12

15

You are counting by 3s!

$$3 + 9 = 12$$

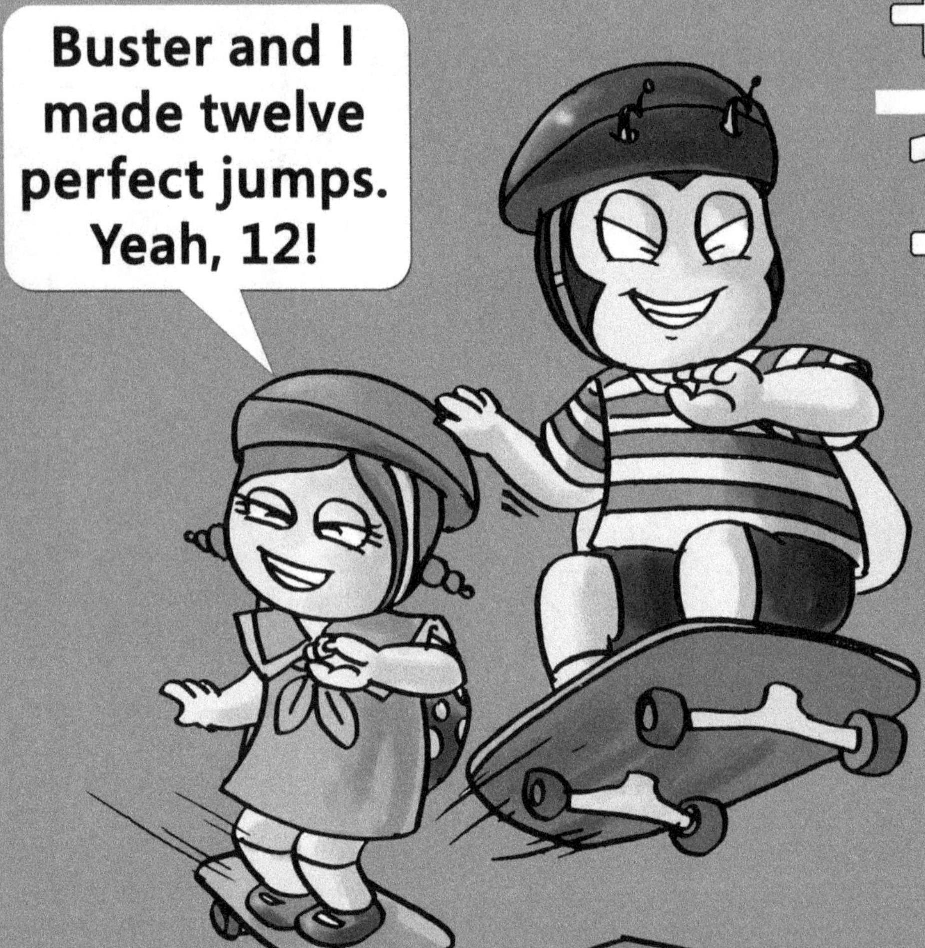

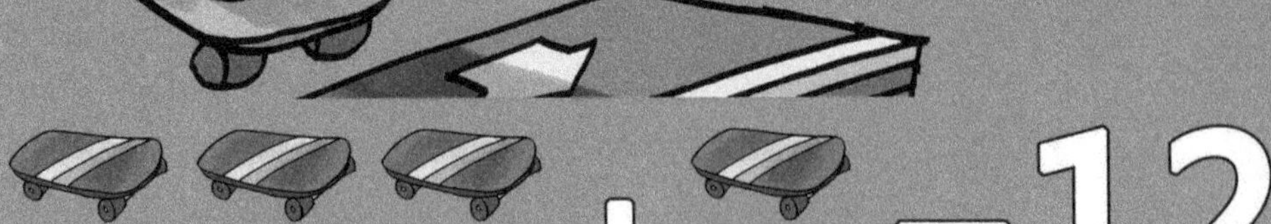

$$\begin{array}{r} 5 \\ +\,7 \\ \hline 12 \end{array}$$

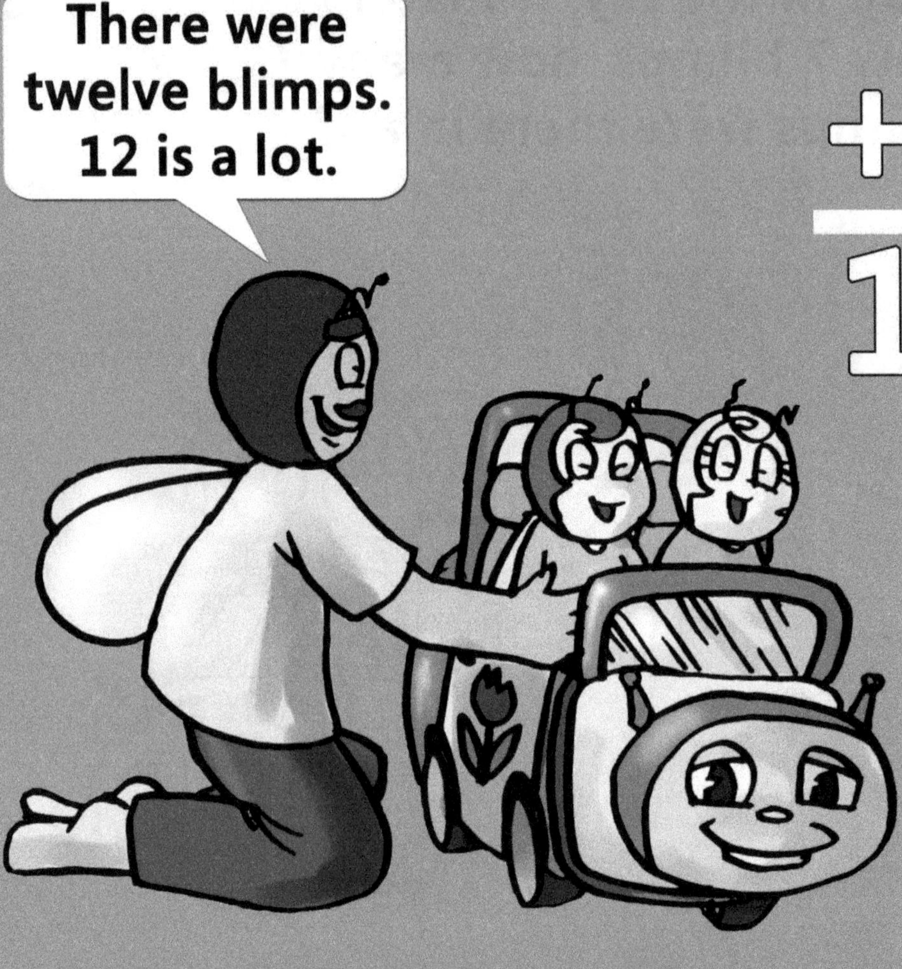

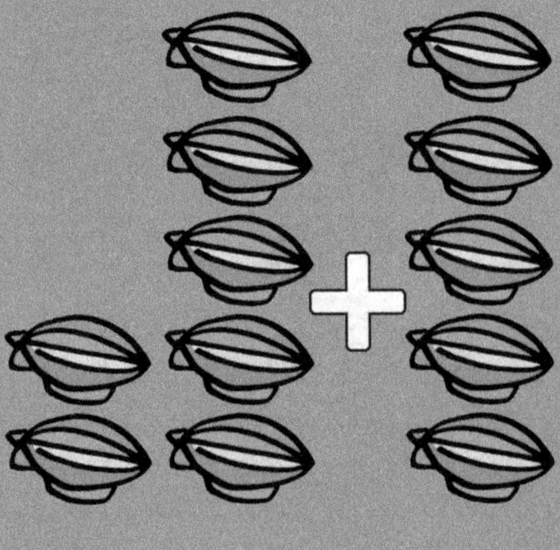

$= \underline{12}$

$$\begin{array}{r} 8 \\ +7 \\ \hline 15 \end{array}$$

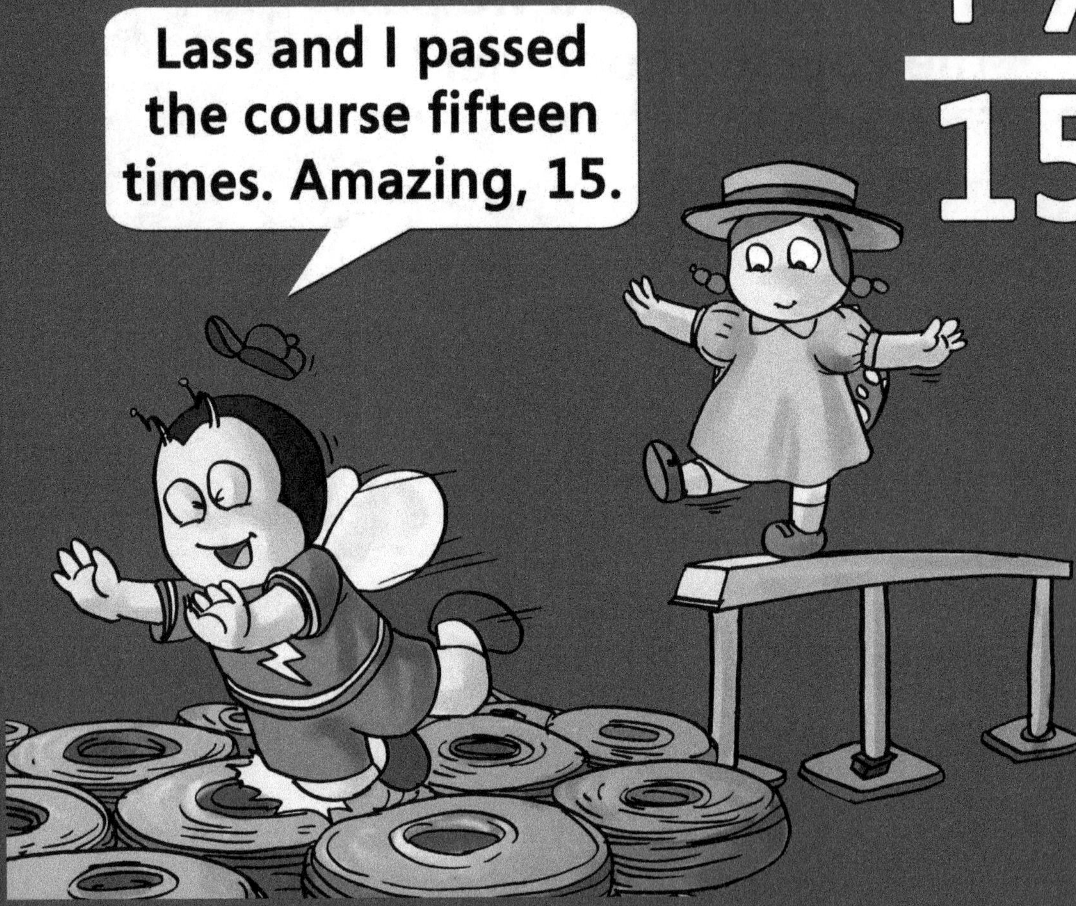

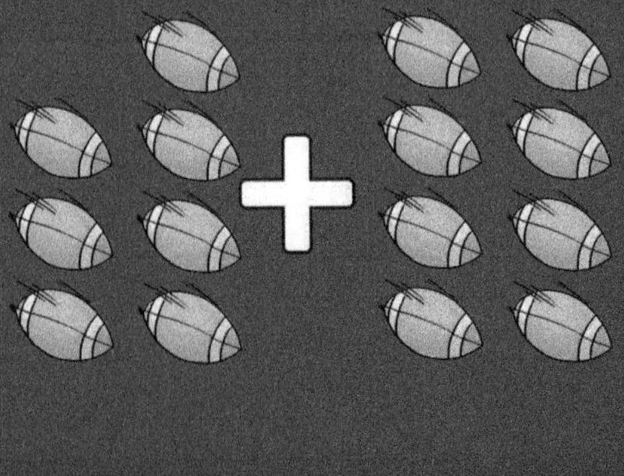

$= \underline{15}$

$$\begin{array}{r} 1 \\ +9 \\ \hline \end{array}$$

I have one toy. If my friend, Barry, gives me 9 more toys, how many toys will I have?

BREAK

BREAK TEASERS

Which two numbers are the closest to 50: 32, 41, 19, 25?

Count up by tens from 10 to 100.

BREAK

ANSWERS

Which two numbers are the closest to 50: 32, 41, 19, 25?	32 and 41
Count up by tens from 10 to 100.	10, 20, 30, 40, 50, 60, 70, 80, 90, 100

MATH SUPER STARS

Graphs can help you compare numbers. Look at this graph.

Answer these questions. Who has the most gold stars?

Who has the least gold stars?

MATH SUPER STARS

Answers:

Buster has the most gold stars. He has 5.

Tim has the least gold stars. He has 3.

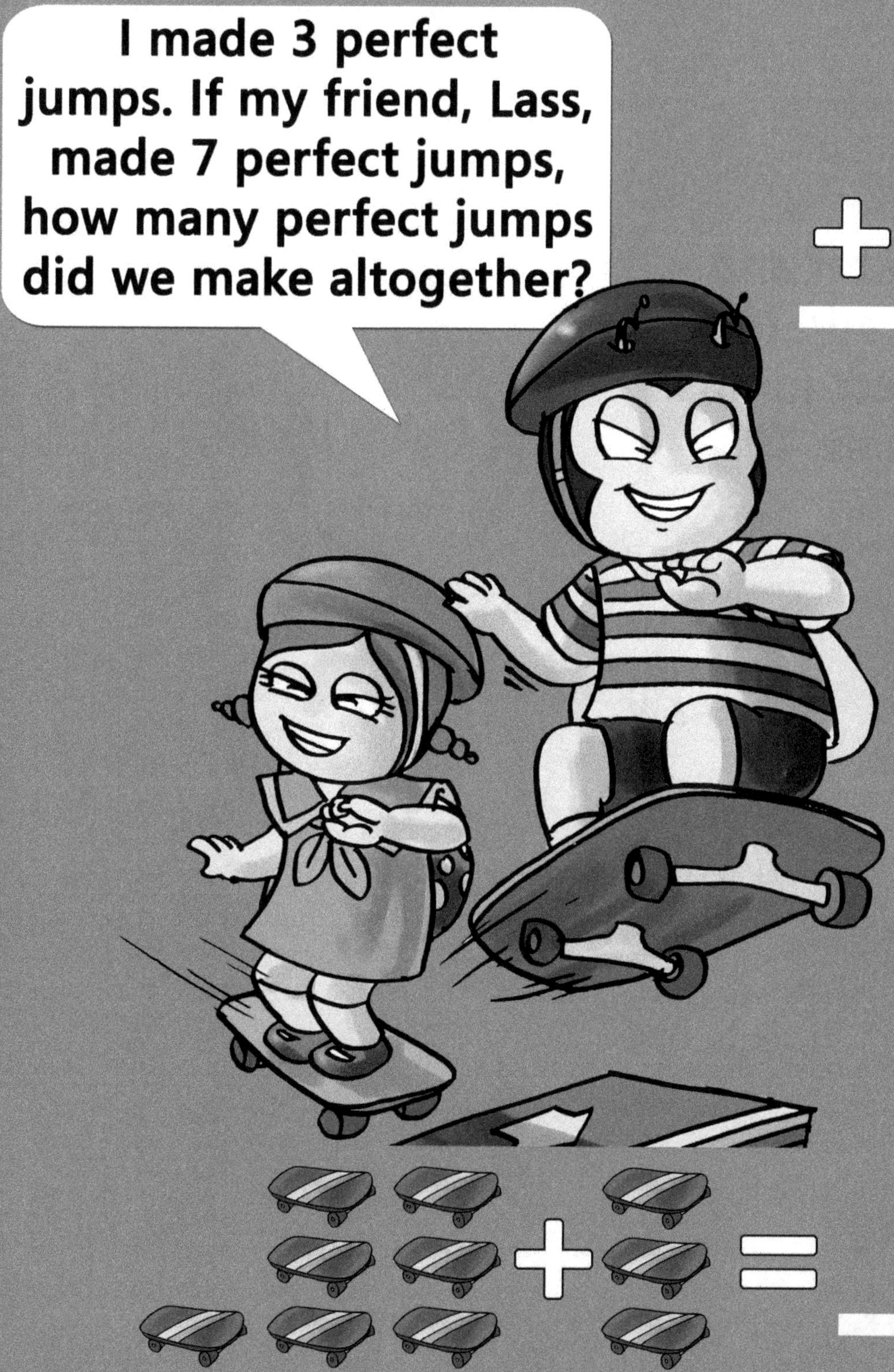

$$\begin{array}{r} 3 \\ +\,7 \\ \hline \end{array}$$

BREAK

BREAK TEASERS

Count up by 5s to 20.

A triangle has fewer sides than a square. True or False?

BREAK

ANSWERS

Count up by 5s to 20.	5, 10, 15, 20
A triangle has fewer sides than a square. True or False?	True (A triangle has 3 sides. A square has 4 sides.)

MATH SUPER STARS

Count the number of robots in each group.

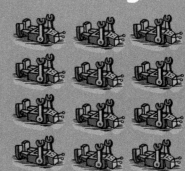

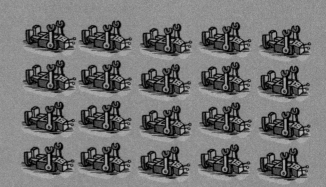

MATH SUPER STARS

Say the answers out loud.

4

8

12

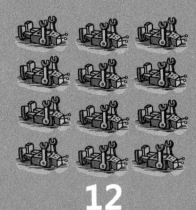

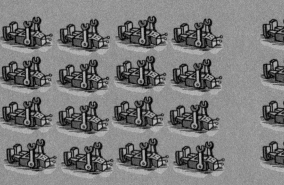

16

20

You are counting by 4s!

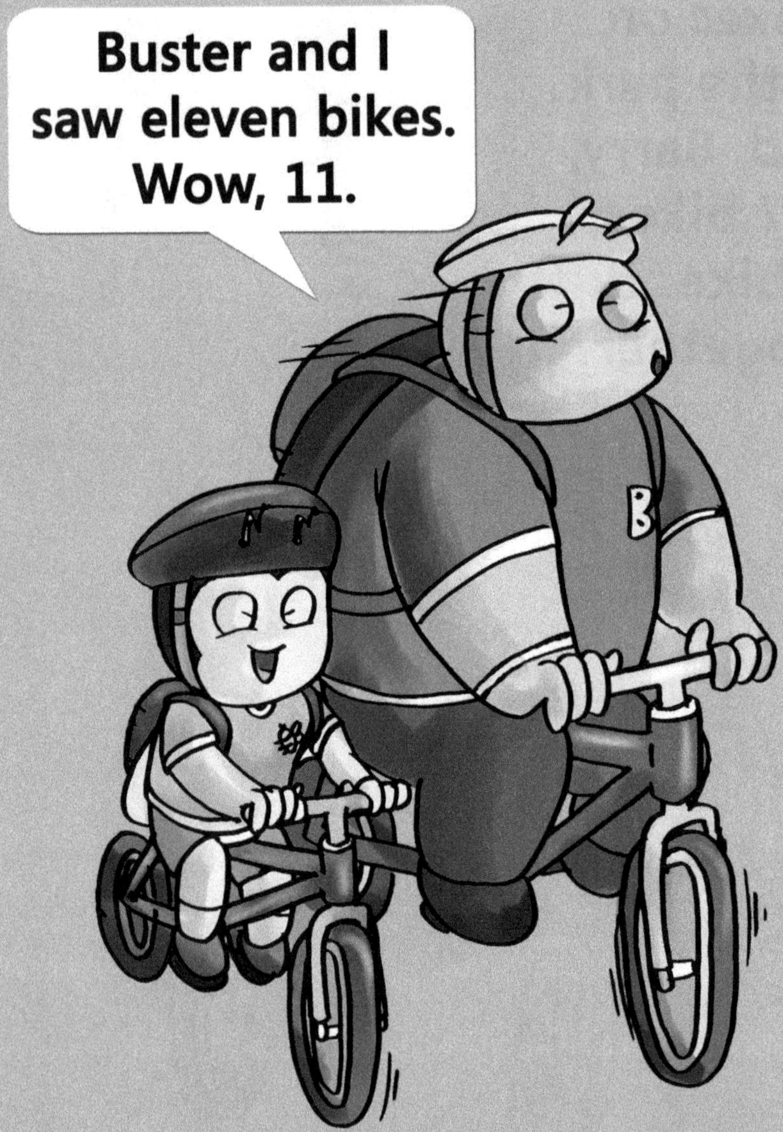

$$\begin{array}{r} 4 \\ +\,7 \\ \hline 11 \end{array}$$

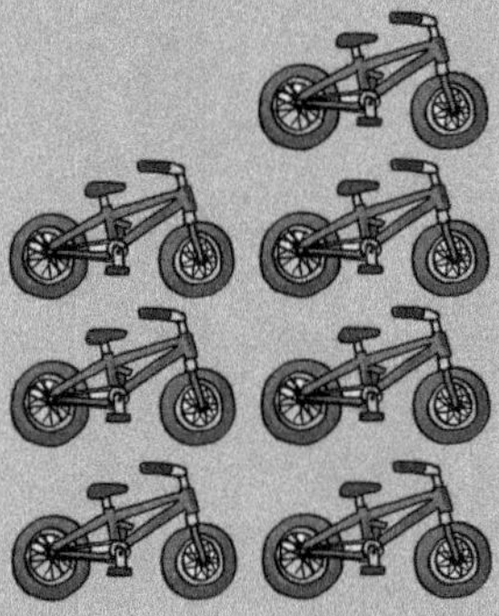 + 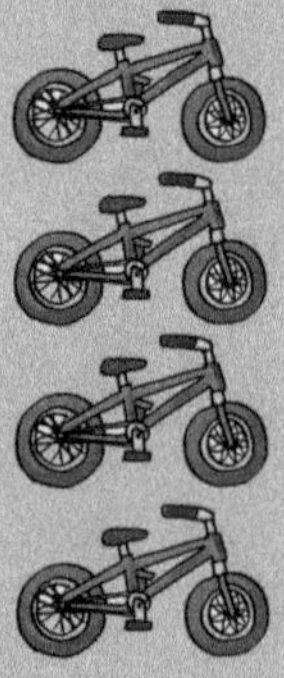 = 11

$$\begin{array}{r} 10 \\ +8 \\ \hline 18 \end{array}$$

There are 18 skaters at the party. Cool, eighteen.

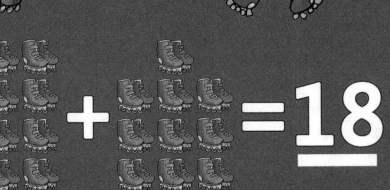

BREAK

BREAK TEASER

Sarah loves origami. She made 3 origami fish, 2 frogs, and 2 swans. How many animals in all?

Find the sum: 19 + 2.

Break

Answers

Sarah loves origami. She made 3 origami fish, 2 frogs, and 2 swans. How many animals in all?	7 (3 + 2 +2 = 7)
Find the sum: 19 + 2.	21

MATH SUPER STARS

Graphs can help you compare numbers. Look at this graph.

Answer these questions. Who has the most gold stars?

Who has the least gold stars?

MATH SUPER STARS

Answers:

Buster has the most gold stars. He has 9.

Lass has the least gold stars. She has 7.

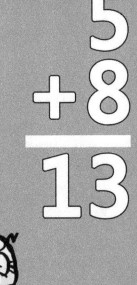

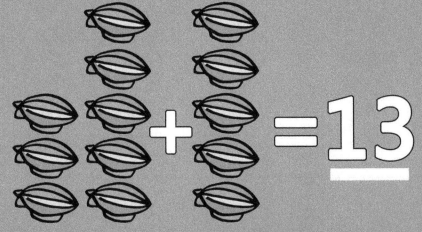

I sold 7 cups of lemonade. If my friend, Lass, sold 9 cups of lemonade, how many cups of lemonade did we sell in all?

$$\begin{array}{r} 7 \\ +\,9 \\ \hline 16 \end{array}$$

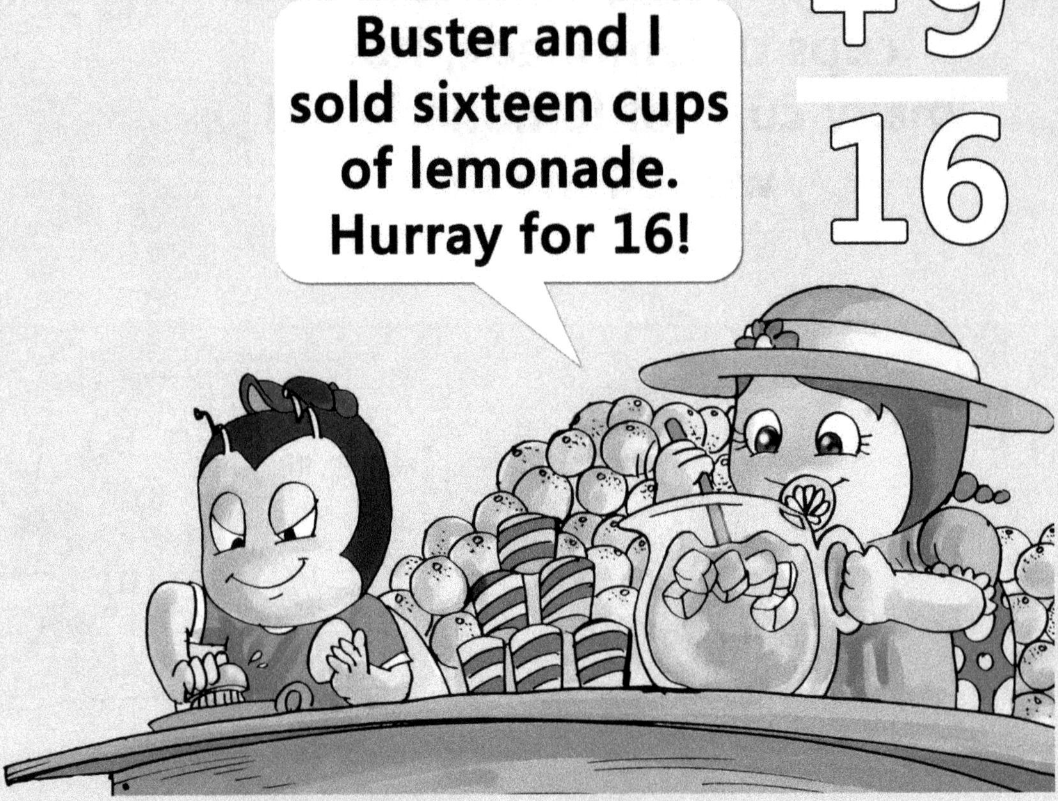

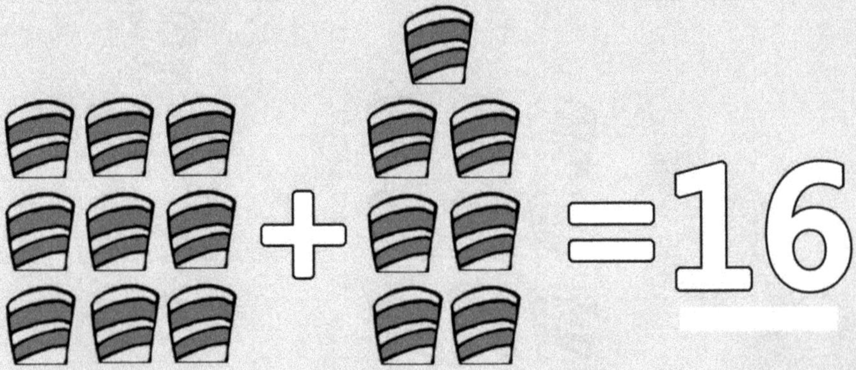

MATH SUPER STARS

You **add** to find out how many things there are in all. Example: 12 + 5 = 17.

Here we are adding the numbers 12 and 5. We use a + sign to show this.

17 is how many we have in all. This is called the **sum**. We use an = sign to show the sum.

Math sentences are called equations. Equations can be written two ways:

$$12 + 9 = 21 \qquad \begin{array}{r} 12 \\ +9 \\ \hline 21 \end{array}$$

MATH SUPER STARS

When you have groups of things, you can count them to determine the sum. Count the skateboards to determine how many there are:

$+$ $=$

The answer is:

$$1 \quad 4 \quad 7 \quad 10$$
$$2 \quad 5 + 8 \quad 11 = 12$$
$$3 \quad 6 \quad 9 \quad 12$$

But also think about how many things are in each group:

6 boards + 6 boards = 12 boards

I sold 7 cups of lemonade. If my friend, Lass, sold 8 cups of lemonade, how many cups of lemonade did we sell in all?

Buster and I sold fifteen cups of lemonade. Hurray for 15!

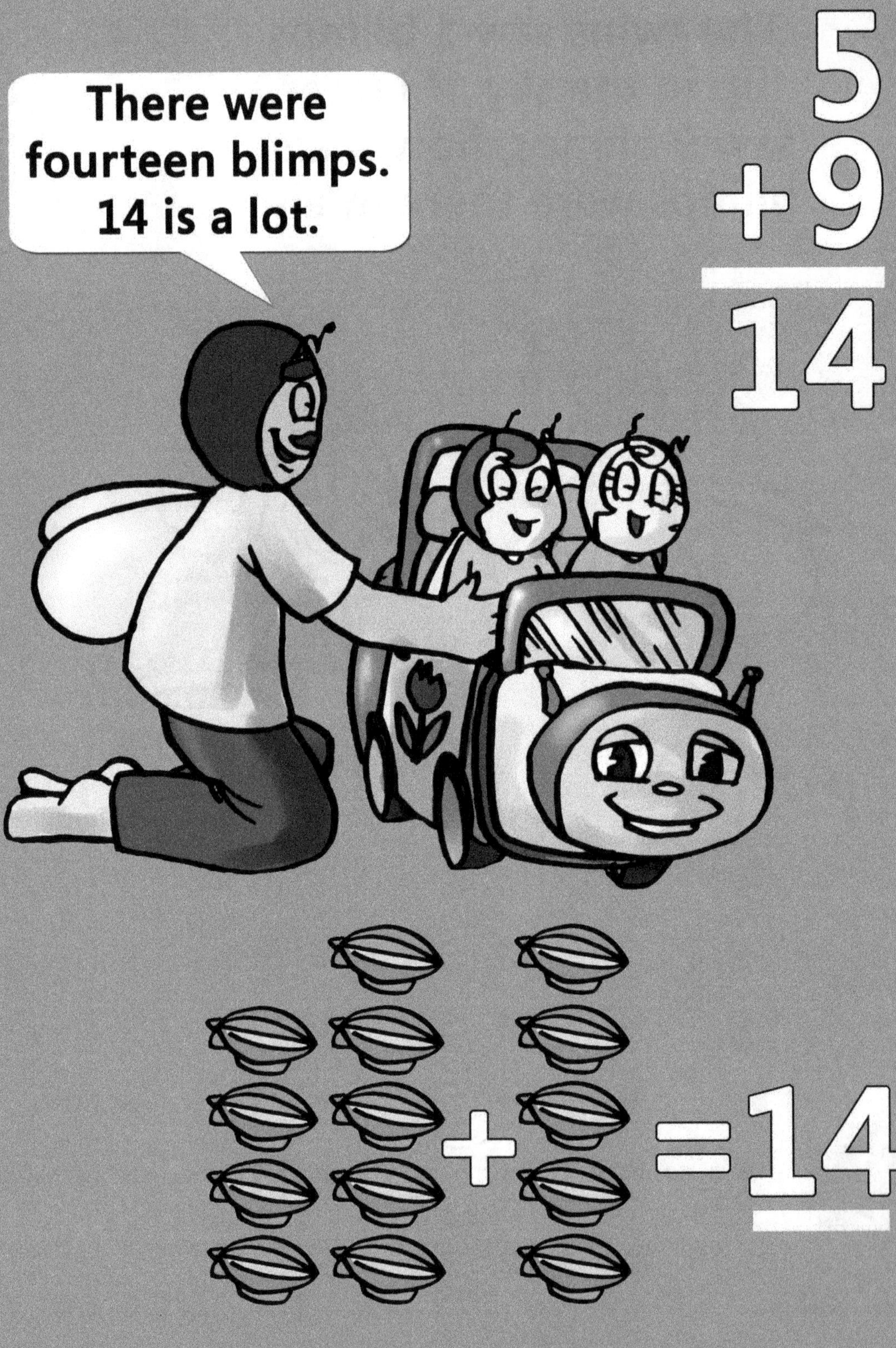
There were fourteen blimps. 14 is a lot.
5
+9
14
+
=14

$$\begin{array}{r} 10 \\ +9 \\ \hline 19 \end{array}$$

$$\begin{array}{r} 2 \\ +8 \\ \hline 10 \end{array}$$

You hit ten baseballs, Buster. 10 sure is a lot!

BREAK

BREAK TEASERS

Would you add or
subtract the numbers
7 and 2 to get 9?

Add 3 to 27. What do
you get?

BREAK

ANSWERS

Would you add or subtract the numbers 7 and 2 to get 9?	Add (7 + 2 = 9)
Add 3 to 27. What do you get?	30 (27 + 3 = 30)

MATH SUPER STARS

Count the number of boats in each group.

MATH SUPER STARS

Say the answers out loud.

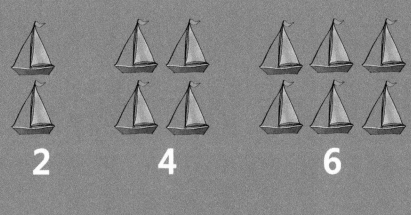

2   4   6

8   10

You are counting by 2s!

$$\begin{array}{r} 10 \\ +7 \\ \hline 17 \end{array}$$

There are 17 skaters at the party. Cool, seventeen.

 $= \underline{17}$

$$\begin{array}{r} 11 \\ +9 \\ \hline \end{array}$$

BREAK

BREAK TEASERS

Lass collected 10 colorful leaves for the Fall Leaf wall. Buster collected 7 leaves. How many leaves in all?

Start with 12 and count ahead 3. What number did you get?

BREAK

ANSWERS

Lass collected 10 colorful leaves for the Fall Leaf wall. Buster collected 7 leaves. How many leaves in all?	17 (10 + 7 = 17)
Start with 12 and count ahead 3. What number did you get?	14 (12, 13, 14)

MATH SUPER STARS

Count the number of bikes in each group.

MATH SUPER STARS

Say the answers out loud.

3

6

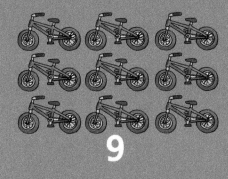

9

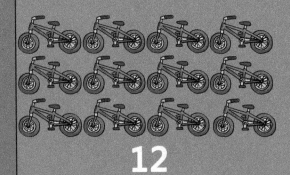

12

15

You are counting by 3s!

$$11$$
$$+8$$
$$\overline{19}$$

I made 3 perfect jumps. If my friend, Lass, made 9 perfect jumps, how many perfect jumps did we make altogether?
3
+9

$$\begin{array}{r} 8 \\ +\,7 \\ \hline 15 \end{array}$$

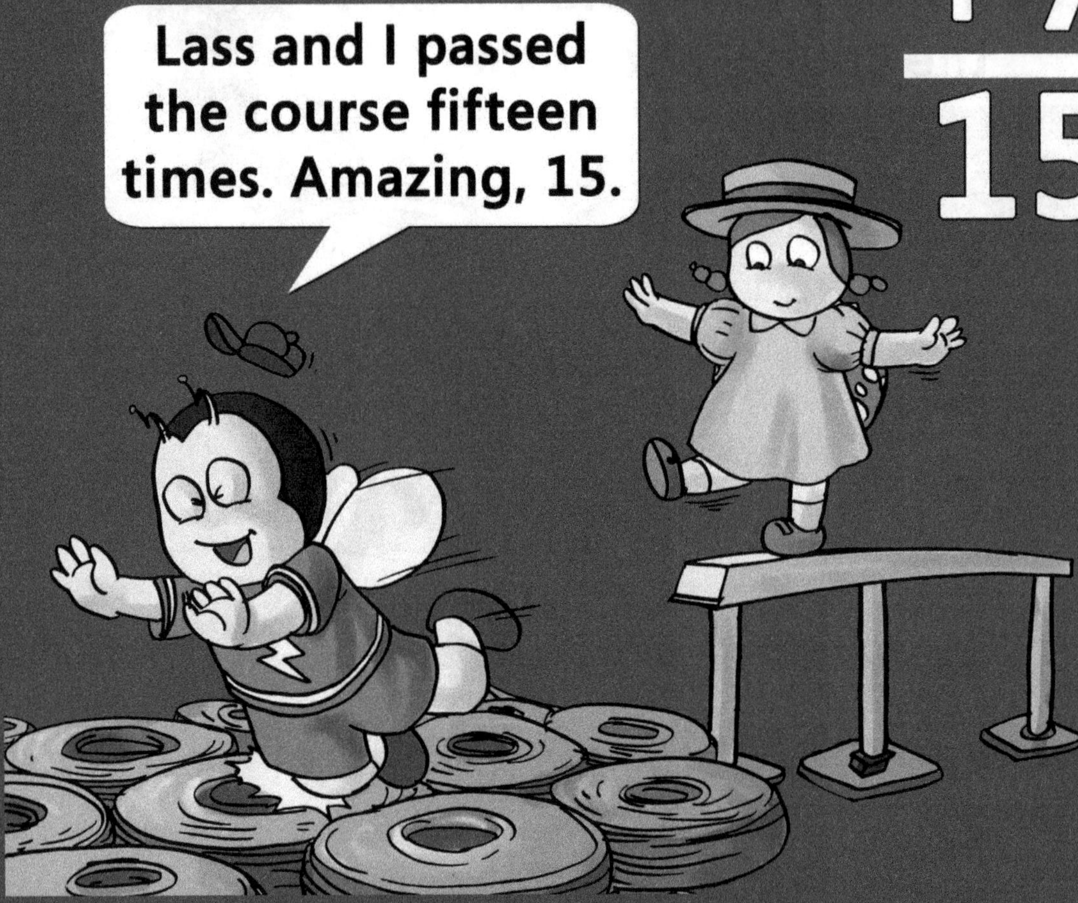

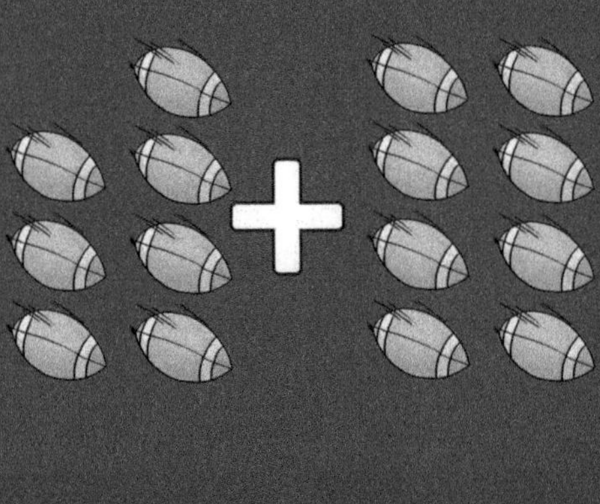

= 15

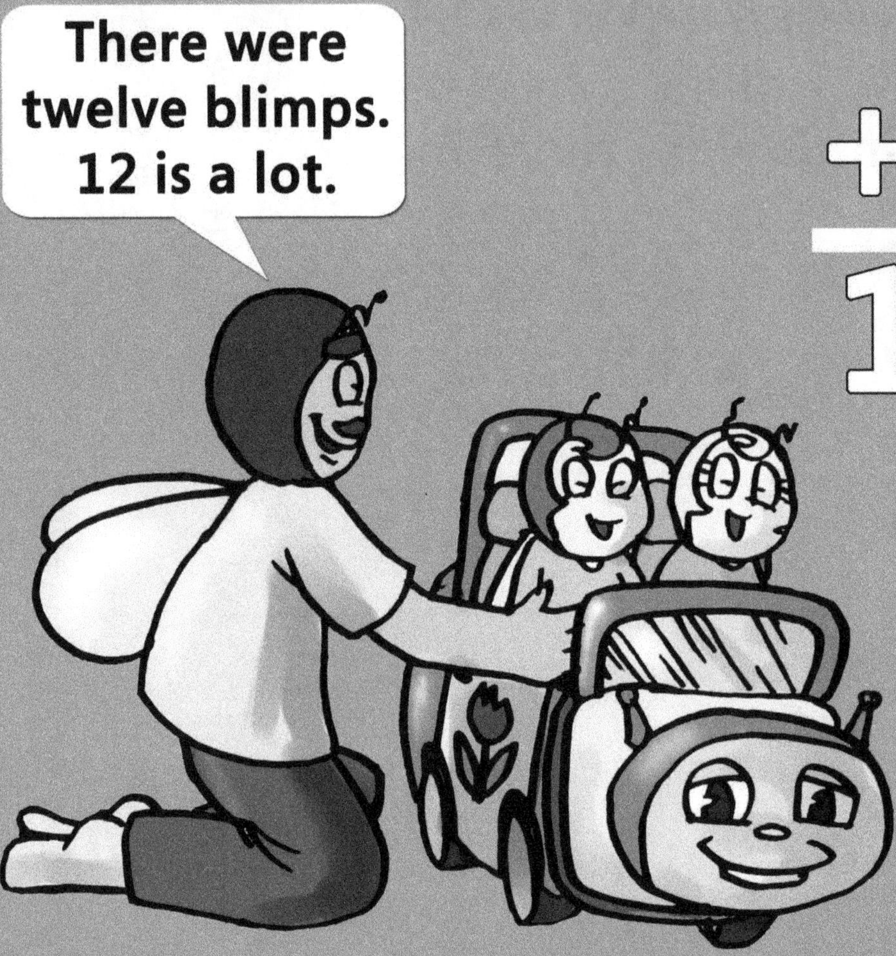

$$\begin{array}{r} 5 \\ +\,7 \\ \hline 12 \end{array}$$

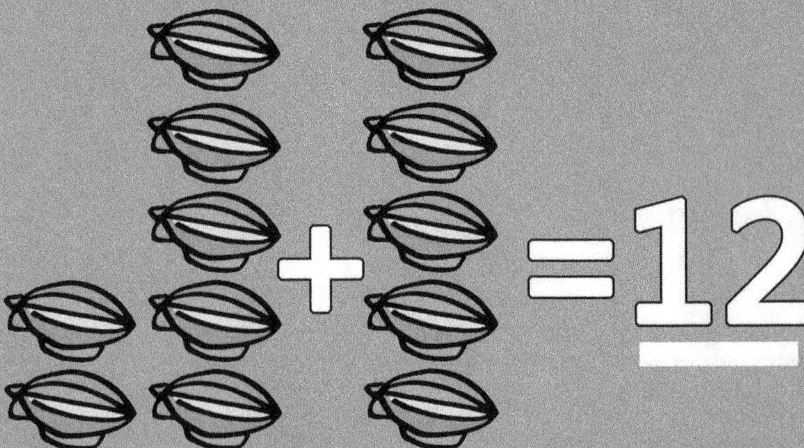

$$\begin{array}{r} 1 \\ +\,9 \\ \hline \end{array}$$

I have one toy. If my friend, Barry, gives me 9 more toys, how many toys will I have?

BREAK

BREAK TEASERS

Which two numbers are the closest to 50: 32, 41, 19, 25?

Count up by tens from 10 to 100.

BREAK

ANSWERS

Which two numbers are the closest to 50: 32, 41, 19, 25?	32 and 41
Count up by tens from 10 to 100.	10, 20, 30, 40, 50, 60, 70, 80, 90, 100

Ready to start your math pratice again?

Sure thing, we're done riding our bikes.

MATH SUPER STARS

Graphs can help you compare numbers. Look at this graph.

Answer these questions. Who has the most gold stars?

Who has the least gold stars?

MATH SUPER STARS

Answers:

Buster has the most gold stars. He has 5.

Tim has the least gold stars. He has 3.

On our first dive, we saw 9 fish. On our second dive, we saw 8 fish. How many fish did we see in all?

I made 3 perfect jumps. If my friend, Lass, made 7 perfect jumps, how many perfect jumps did we make altogether?
3
+7
+
=

BREAK

BREAK TEASERS

Count up by 5s to 20.

A triangle has fewer sides than a square. True or False?

Count up by 5s to 20.	5, 10, 15, 20
A triangle has fewer sides than a square. True or False?	True (A triangle has 3 sides. A square has 4 sides.)

MATH SUPER STARS

Count the number of robots in each group.

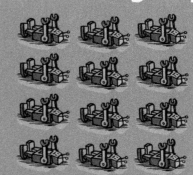

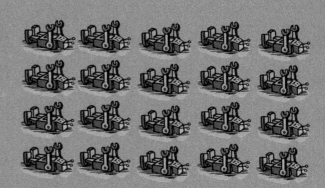

MATH SUPER STARS

Say the answers out loud.

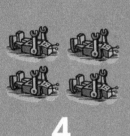

4

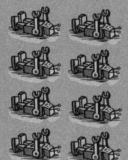

8

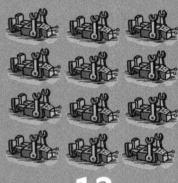

12

16

20

You are counting by 4s!

$$\begin{array}{r} 10 \\ +8 \\ \hline 18 \end{array}$$

There are 18 skaters at the party. Cool, eighteen.

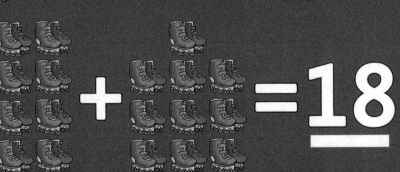

$$\begin{array}{r} 8 \\ +\,9 \\ \hline 17 \end{array}$$

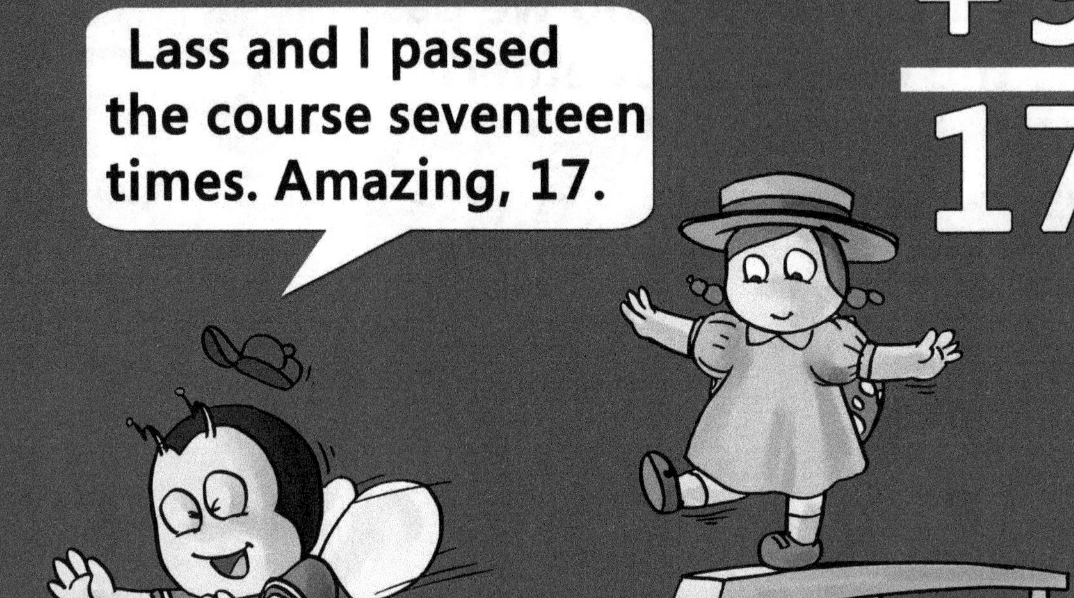

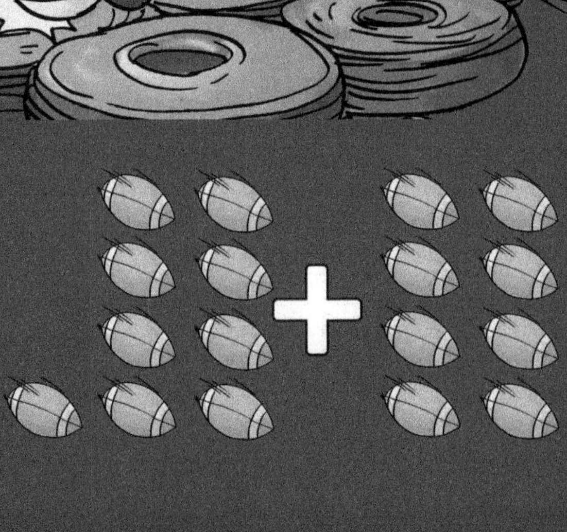

$= \underline{17}$

BREAK

BREAK TEASER

Sarah loves origami. She made 3 origami fish, 2 frogs, and 2 swans. How many animals in all?

Find the sum: 19 + 2.

BREAK

ANSWERS

Sarah loves origami. She made 3 origami fish, 2 frogs, and 2 swans. How many animals in all?

7 (3 + 2 +2 = 7)

Find the sum: 19 + 2.

21

MATH SUPER STARS

Graphs can help you compare numbers. Look at this graph.

Answer these questions. Who has the most gold stars?

Who has the least gold stars?

MATH SUPER STARS

Answers:

Buster has the most gold stars. He has 9.

Lass has the least gold stars. She has 7.

I sold 7 cups of lemonade. If my friend, Lass, sold 9 cups of lemonade, how many cups of lemonade did we sell in all?

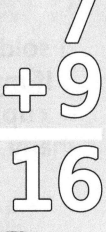

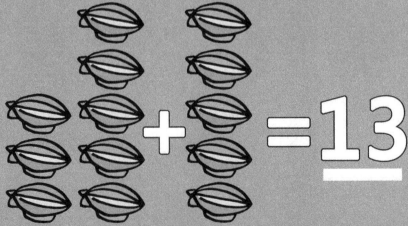

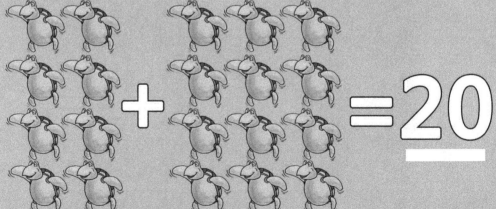

CPSIA information can be obtained
at www.ICGtesting.com
Printed in the USA
BVHW051756270321
603568BV00012B/1281